ELEVEN GARDEN TYPES

Formal, Naturalistic, and Wild

Dénes D. Boronkay
Dr. Juris, B.L.S.
Learned Landscape Gardener

Note for Librarians: a cataloguing record for this book that includes Dewey Decimal Classification and US Library of Congress numbers is available from the Library and Archives of Canada. The complete cataloguing record can be obtained from their online database at: www.collectionscanada.ca/amicus/index-e.html
ISBN 1-4120-5846-5

Cover Photo, 2004, "Smiling Corner", Vermont

Printed on paper with minimum 30% recycled fibre.
Trafford's print shop runs on "green energy" from solar, wind and other environmentally-friendly power sources.

TRAFFORD

Offices in Canada, USA, Ireland and UK
This book was published *on-demand* in cooperation with Trafford Publishing. On-demand publishing is a unique process and service of making a book available for retail sale to the public taking advantage of on-demand manufacturing and Internet marketing. On-demand publishing includes promotions, retail sales, manufacturing, order fulfilment, accounting and collecting royalties on behalf of the author.

Book sales for North America and international:
Trafford Publishing, 6E–2333 Government St.,
Victoria, BC v8t 4p4 CANADA
phone 250 383 6864 (toll-free 1 888 232 4444)
fax 250 383 6804; email to orders@trafford.com
Book sales in Europe:
Trafford Publishing (uk) Ltd., Enterprise House, Wistaston Road Business Centre,
Wistaston Road, Crewe, Cheshire cw2 7rp UNITED KINGDOM
phone 01270 251 396 (local rate 0845 230 9601)
facsimile 01270 254 983; orders.uk@trafford.com
Order online at:
trafford.com/05-0746
10 9 8 7 6 5 4 3 2 1

PREFACE

GARDENS in the first quarter of the twenty-first century? Certainly. And even more so in the next two quarters of the century if you dare to contemplate the odds what our descendants or we will be up to. The more things get troublesome around and with us, the more our human species will need some kind of get-away place; sunny or shady nook, a tucked-away wooded corner, or a flowery meadow to communicate with Nature, to keep physical strength and emotional life in a healthy state, and to dream human dreams.

I would even put the dreams in the first place because they last all through the calendar year irrespective of the so-called growing season between the last frost in the spring, and the first one in the fall. They even get stronger and more colourful in the dreary part of the year, and our hope will never fail to insinuate from the second half of November on that **with every day that spring is coming closer**.

Everybody is more contented with the physical surroundings of our globe since we had a frustrated look at the moon. The more surprising is the fact that so small use is made of the opportunities which has been offered to a fortunately placed humanity.

Should not be taught from the start of school age on all through the educational process the multiple ways open to us, and the means at our disposal to work and live with what has so carefully, cleverly, and abundantly been put at our arm's length, at our hand's reach, and at our feet's touch? How many facts, concepts, and theories are crammed in youthful minds which they never encounter again in adult life;

why not instill in their ready soul susceptibilities to the interest, attractions, and beauty which will be their accompaniment on a smaller or larger scale anywhere they will happen to live?

Especially on the North American continent the sources of potential human satisfaction are so bountiful that this may be one of the reasons why they are passed by unnoticed and unused by so many. Also, the comforts of an apartment taste better after the bones and muscles have been through kinds of active use, and deserve some recovery afterwards. Entertaining ourselves in a passive way does not measure up to the advantages derived from active pastimes. Then, financial considerations too could but should not necessarily enter into the minds, which exert their resourcefulness in gardening.

But gardening should not be thought of in a restricted sense because Nature is generous, and responds n this same generous spirit to any kind of approach to deal with any of her excellencies, be it flower or shrub, grass or tree, waterscape or landscape. Neither is spading the only treatment, which should be considered indispensable for becoming a gardener. Hillock and hollow, pasture and pine grove, ferns and flowers, paths and pruning, dells and ditches, brooks and bumps, rocks and ravines, mould and mountains, scenery and sky, all and many more will offer plenty of thought and activity to the one who cares.

The possibilities for gardening therefore are manyfold. Gardening may be a flowerpot on a windowsill if you are above age or homebound, or else it may be a hillside glorious with sheets of colour if your energies are still with you. There may be a plot or two in the backyard to look at the flowers in them, it may be a shrub border with spring bulbs underneath cheerfully breaking through the snow, it may be a few fruit trees to pamper with, or just varied natural grounds to walk around.

In what style do you arrange the composing parts and features of your place is immaterial provided it is congruous with the surroundings, and answer to the need of the uses to which you intend to submit the place. Your preferences should suggest your choices, but if you study the underlying principles of good taste which have long been evolved to the compositions of different sorts of gardens and grounds as safely leading to success you will not be tempted to a trial and error process, and likely to encounter failure.

Formal or naturalistic, rock or wild, and any other type of gardens and grounds correspond to the disposition of our souls and to the requirements of their sites. Every one of them is beautiful and satisfying on its own right, and enjoyable including those in favour maybe of another style, but the same gardens would be out of place if forced on sites which would be uncongenial to the specific beauties inherent in different forms in any of them.

What are then, the requisites of good taste to be thought of before, during, and even after our creations?

CONTENTS

PREFACE

CHAPTER I

A Formal Garden

"Round the house… a formal garden….;
and in this … only convenience, grace and
elegance … we desire."

Pückler-Muskau

GEORGE and LOUISE have just returned from
Australia, after several years stay in Melbourne due to
George's official assignment there. Louise's former
classmate, Nellie, has faithfully corresponded with her
friend during these years so that Louise has been
informed about the new home where Nellie and her
husband, Richard had settled over two years before.
She has been thrilled at the prospect to go over, and
see her old friends, and their new home when soon
after their arrival Nellie rang her up with an invitation
to spend a weekend afternoon with them.

The warmth of their reception has been as it could
have been expected for a welcome meeting, and after
the initial few minutes of mutual pleasantries, Nellie
has taken her friend by her arm, and has led her into
the living room. Louise has suddenly stopped in
front of the picture window. "My! What a beautiful
garden picture! How could you have made such a
charming garden! I am simply fascinated by it, what a
really pleasing view." (See following illustration)

1

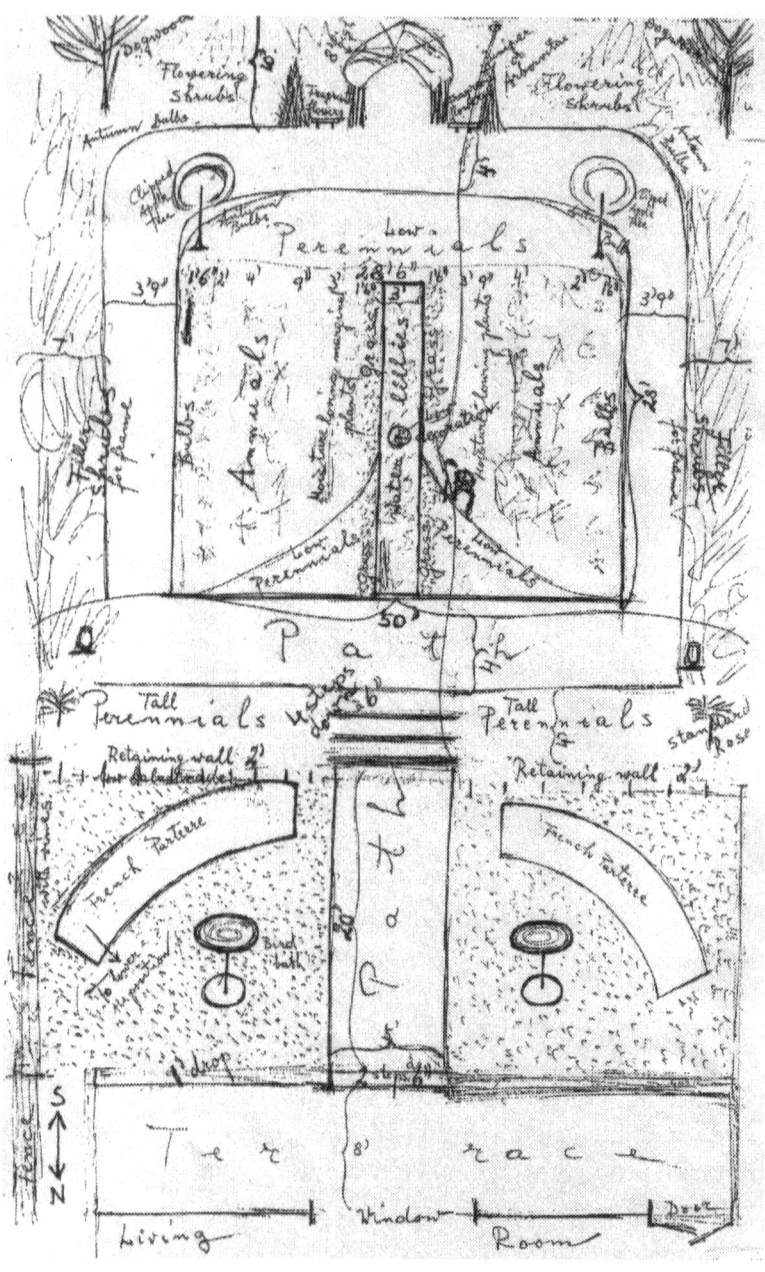

"Thank you, Louise, I knew that you would have appreciation for it. You will still hear a lot about it from me because this has successively become my favorite subject. As a matter of fact, I cannot detach my thoughts from this garden."

"I can well understand it, Nellie, and I shall be a good listener because I should like to follow in your steps, now that we are at home again, and hopefully shall stay too."

"Well, as you can sense by looking at it, this is a fairly narrow lot considering the length of it, some 50 by 140 feet out of which the garden occupies the whole width at the back of the house, and 70 feet of the length. These could be considered otherwise to be good proportions for a formal garden."

"Formal, to be sure, but I do not feel any stiff regularity, any rigidity of geometrical lines about it."

"This is one of the major secrets, Louise. The geometrical base is there, but superimposed on it is a kind of free growing luxuriance of vegetation, with accent plants only at the strategic points in order to bring out and hold together the formal arrangement. Right from here you can see the two Dogwood trees located in the far end where they point up the boundary corners. Then, nearer to us you see the round-clipped small apple trees, followed by closer standing pyramidal junipers, and in the middle of them the summer shelter as terminal feature of the main garden axis, flanked by seats. These also serve the perspective which has been introduced by the main path down the foreground section of the garden, followed by the water-lily canal

3

in the second section, effectively assisted by the parallel running grass margin on both sides of it."

"How come that the shelter seems to be closer than the 68 feet where it actually is from where we stand?"

"Because of the middle ground treatment if I may call it so. Should there be no intermediate features between us and the terminal shelter in the second garden section, and only a foreground jumping off for our view from the first section the shelter would look farther off than it actually does in our case. And those nice details on our elongated garden plan have created added attractions to enjoy while our eyes are led further along to the terminal point of our picture."

"This is really interesting."

"Also, the change of levels between the two garden sections causes a certain shortening of distance in our view. Should the garden be laid out on one sloping ground this would lengthen the distance of it in our vision. Then, the framing of our picture by the filler shrubs certainly has a marked effect on this enclosed and shortened view."

"You talk like a landscape designer, Nellie."

"Well, that is what I have been up to since you left us Louise, because I had to find some replacement for a lost image, you know."

"Thank you, Nellie, I shall try hard to climb back into the frame of your image again."

"You have been in my image from the very first moment of your reappearance, my dear, especially

4

now that I can see you in the frame of my garden picture."

"I see. Strange enough but I do not feel like crying rather, I shall join you in your gardening interest."

"My dear, dear Louise." Kiss on the cheek; kiss on the other cheek.

"Now, in order to initiate you further into the principals of garden craft, Louise, stay here in the window for a while, and look at the garden picture. **Lines** are supposed to be predominant in the formal type as against the details of whatever planting is enclosed within them. Even though the lines to be used in the creation of the forms cannot offer a great variety still, you can put in them a combination of some character, and show by them something of your personality. These for instance represent **my** lines Louise, straight, segments of the circle, and roundish … I mean, these are the lines of my garden formally treated."

"Yes, Nellie, but I **do** find them somehow fitting to you if you do not mind. Richard must find them to **his** liking too."

"But Louise, please do not make a joke out of my lay-out. There are other advantages to these lines too, Louise because they stay there even when the flowering, or the flourishing season for that matter are over. They are steady, and give you solace and continued aesthetic enjoyment. The birdbaths with the curved beds of the French parterres, the balustrades at the division line, the paths and steps, the perennial beds, the canal with the grass margins, the round-headed apple trees, the pyramidal junipers, and the low benches with the pleasing structure between them all have their effect on you. Also the frame of the picture, fence and balustrade, shrubs and corner accents continue to hold together your visual possession, and present it right here to the windows, rain or shine, calm or windy.

Beside the enframing, artistic treatment would also require **segregation** of your picture or pictures, and that is one of the main reasons why I have taken advantage of the slight drop in the ground which existed where the steps are now located. I had it slightly deepened in order to have the two feet variation in the levels. This had created other results too beside the demarcation of the garden areas, one good, and one not so good although not a really bad one either.

For one, the foreground section has a reposeful atmosphere. We can sit out like in an extension room out-of-doors. It is well delineated, and enclosed in a kind of sheltering privacy. Besides, the grass surfaces and back fences with the vines act as good foil to the flowers in the parterres. Actually, the very smallness of this section of the garden makes for coziness.

On the other hand, should the partition line between the two garden sections be some 30 feet further, i.e., the proportions of the two garden areas would this way be in reversed order, that would induce the onlookers to think that the garden is bisected by the transversal line of the change of level. Therefore, the garden would look larger to them that it actually would be. With the existing sequence of the two sections this deluding effect we could not introduce, and it may be better this way because I do not like to fool my guests into delusions.

I can tell you some more reasons, Louise why I like and prefer the proportions as they are. Beside the coziness of the nearer section I have a better chance to indulge in having many more flowers, bulbs, annuals, and marginal plants in masses in the second area, and get a really good effect out of them this way. Also, I have more walking space in the farther away part, at a distance from the house where this kind of activity really belongs.

To get there I follow the path right from our terrace, and this way a direct connection is established between the house and garden which is important in the case of formally treated gardens. This connection is continued on the line of vision by the water-lily canal, and path and canal together form the all-important main longitudinal **axis** of the composition. The axis is terminated, as all axes should be, with a closing feature, in our case with a shelter, which is in proportionately happy relation with this axis, its 8 feet height being approximately a tenth part of the whole axis length from window to shelter.

You can also notice, Louise that the perennial bed in the middle of the second garden area points toward the center decoration of the canal, and further on with its directional line toward the shelter. It gives added strength this way to the lead of the main axis towards its important terminal feature. It also calls attention to the water lilies. I find that this feature has a unifying effect for the whole composition.

Termination is also needed for any **cross axes** but these being minor in importance should have a lesser object in size and effect than the major axis. Therefore, two vases serve this purpose at the ends of the cross axis running below the steps, and have altogether been made superfluous by the rounding off of the corners on both sides of the turning of the second cross path at the end of the garden.

Coming back to the main axis for a moment, the decoration in the middle of the canal had been kept **low** as you can see, so as not to interrupt the line of vision along the axis. And so it is as it should be.

With the canal and its grass margins an open stretch has been kept through the center of the second garden section. This arrangement has enabled me to gather my flowers in the middle parts of the whole plot rather than toward the margins only. This way I could secure the beauty of intensified mass effect in their colours, forms, and textures, and let the sun strike them longer by the avoidance of shading by the shrubs from the sides in the morning and afternoon hours as they would be shaded if the plantings were toward the margins of the plot. The garden lays in a north-south direction as you can see marked on the illustration.

The flowers being important as they are for me I have deviated by their arrangement from a canon of formal gardening, and have gained several advantages thereby. I just have mentioned two of these advantages. Furthermore, by keeping most of the flowers together I do not have to strain myself for orderliness in their treatment, and gain thereby a cottage-garden type effect of a formally laid out garden. True, the flower decoration is not as simple as by strict application of the cardinal rule for simplicity of arrangement it should be. I have to admit that. On the other hand, a certain intricacy had been introduced in the garden picture this way, which I find more pleasing in its variety, and which gives an all-together more picturesque treatment to my pleasure.

To the same effect, freely developing shrubs have been used rather than clipped hedges without loosing thereby the charm of a formal garden. By the same token, with the height of the frame formed by these same shrubs and the accent points at the strategically important locations of the formal plan any flat appearance has been avoided in the garden picture, and I think we have succeeded well with the contour line of the elevations.
By the way, in order to gain a good near view too, the terrace has been built fairly but not uncomfortably narrow to avoid the foreshortening of our view of the lawn with all what that beautiful green carpet means to us in any weather except when snow covers the ground."

"Nellie, if I may interrupt your enthusiastic discourse for a moment, you do **elevate** my garden spirit above the contours of the highest points in the whole picture, believe me."

"Thanks, Louise, we can sit down together at that elevated point for awhile now, and look down to our picture. Actually, this is what we do from our attic. You come with me upstairs, and see how a formal garden gains in effect, and presents itself in clearly grasped compositional best from above."

They hurry up the staircase full with expectations, Nellie to **show,** and Louise to **see** something added to their aesthetic enjoyment.

"You see what I mean, Louise, the layout of the whole garden is visible at once, and with an intensified effect because of the focusing of our eyes by the external frame of fence and shrub. And how the garden gains in depth by the terracing of the two areas, clearly defined at their change of elevations. By terrace side and balustrade the lines of separation are unmistakably defined.

The rest of the pattern is just as clearly discernable, with the varied features in full harmony, and the emphatic points properly pointed up. The darker tones of shrub and juniper enhance the bright colours of the flowers, and the unplanted clear spaces of the water lend a mirror to their beauty, and to the smile of the sky.

The balance of a symmetrical arrangement is felt at the first glance, and to my taste, also the proportion of open and planted areas is satisfactorily solved, although the weight may slightly be put on the plantings, which is in accordance with my special interest in them therefore, pardonable.

The French parterres too show more clearly from here their special beauty in the sunlit smooth green foil of the surrounding grass. And to make the happy picture even happier birds have just alighted on the rim of their bath. Louise, **this** is the place where I have found true happiness."

"Nellie, dear friend, I am fully and thoroughly convinced of the merits of a formally laid out garden, of **your** garden, and of yourself. God bless you with a long season, and thereafter, be buried with the proper **formalities** within these beautiful confines."

"Thank you, Louise, and I do hope that you will join me in everything as soon as you can. But I do not mean that you would have to be buried here, you know."

"Please accept my **formal** apology, dear."

CHAPTER II

Roses in the Garden

"Roslein, Roslein, Roslein rot,
Roslein auf der Heide"
Goethe

AROUND 100 Anno Domini, Plutarch advised to plant the roses with cabbages in order to better bring out the beauty of the former by contrast. Man's taste has markedly changed in the arrangement of his favorite flower during the past nineteen hundred years. But how could the Greek moralist and biographer have foreseen such a development for the years we live in as to rather plant cauliflowers with cabbages because we could easily get roses for the price of one cauliflower. This is not to despise the value of utility plants, only to revoke that advice of olden times, and adjust it by asking you to plant at least a few roses with the cauliflowers in order to save our face before posterity. Otherwise, as many years from now, we could not stand a favourable comparison, and might draw a derogating judgment from the hydroponic gardeners working in closely built-up surroundings. Fortunately enough, we will not be around by that time.

In the meantime, we should be amazed and genuinely pleased while looking around on this wide continent how bountifully sprang up all over the places our "Roslein auf der Heide," the **wild rose** of North America. And I think, it has set an example to us not to be too formal with our planting of roses, although a rose garden as such somehow requires the designing along formal lines, and a formal layout.

Garden roses require careful tending on a properly chosen and segregated place of their jealous own. Narrow beds in ample grass surroundings, in the frame of dark conifers, tall hedge shrubs, but in open enough situations to enjoy the sun with plenty of fresh air are perquisites for garden roses in order to have them fully enjoy their setting then, to give of their best.

A sunken part of the garden scheme further enhances the beauty of the roses but enframes them into even more formality. This formal arrangement is developed again by the careful juxtapostion of chosen colours, and of subjects with compatible habits. Also, the selection of varieties could and should contribute to our appreciation of symmetry in the formally balanced design of a rose garden.

Sculptural decoration in a terminal or central position would add to the formal beauty, and to the mood of this specially set apart place which because of its self-sufficiency does not require it to be in close proximity to the house. The more so because a rose garden does not offer much to appreciative eyes when their chief attractions are not in their flourishing best. Then, the somewhat barren look of their ground could just as well be farther away from the windows. This disconnected location from the dwelling is an exception to the principals of lying out formally treated ground, and is explained and justified by the peculiarities of a separate rose garden. Here, Hybrid Perpetuals, Hybrid Teas, Bengals, Polyanthas, Floribundas, and Grandifloras, in southern climates also Tea roses find their home, and may be looking up to some climbers planted around them.

The **wild rose's suggestion** is for naturalness and spontaneousness, for abundance in flowers and leaves, for the freedom of the arching sprays and of the flowing masses, for carefree roses in the forms of shrub, creeper, and climber. Roses can do everything, and more of it. The flowering season will definitely outlast your holiday, and instead of white-dressed girls in a long greeting-line roses in force will welcome you on all the remaining courageous week-ends then, beautiful red hips in the fall. Still, you will be electrified by looking at the climbers along the fence and on the porch trellis, and would start right on your crawling pastime at the first glimpse of the spreading creepers.

In this wild, rambling way, instead of single or double blooms you will have clusters of smaller roses, and these will be freer from insects and diseases. For dressier grounds the double varieties will be fitting, and for more outlying parts your choice would rather be for single roses.

Should you want to keep more and more leisure time for other summer programs than gardening the Wichuraina class of memorial roses would have a special appeal with their multiple uses, self-sowing habit, and bright green, glossy, and nearly evergreen foliage. Above all this, their flowers, mind you, roses will be offered to you all through the summer, from July to September.

Should you like the whiffs of fragrance, the musk rose, Rosa moschata would produce them with white flowers of a long blooming season, or else the sweetbriar roses with their fragrant foliage.

With roses in the garden you will discover the truth of what somebody said at an earlier day, that with roses planted in the home grounds you will have the jewels set in the garden ring.

CHAPTER III

Patio Garden

WHOEVER HAS a patio garden does not frequently leave his home unless into the patio. There he is just as much at home, protected and surrounded on all sides by the building, by walls and fences or by a loggia. The Romans in their atrium, the medieval monks in their monastic enclosures, and the Moors and Spanish in their Little Paradise have all shared the same feeling of shelter and quiet enjoyment. An enframed and paved sunny courtyard with a center fountain, an orderly arrangement of simples and herbs with intermittent prayers and meditations, or shaded seats with bowers and fragrance in a refreshened atmosphere of leafage and water, these were that attributes of a patio garden, possibly surrounded with a covered passageway.

Modern applications do not deviate much from the essentials of their original models except in the furnishings, and the decorative details and adjuncts maybe. California is not so far from Pompeii as we may think, only instead of the fall of ashes and the flow of lava they have to contend with the periodic rumblings of earthquakes. But again, these calamities can better be encountered from within a roofless patio.

The enclosed space of a patio is really a room pushed out of the house in order to enjoy fresh air from above. Here it is easier to create a homelike atmosphere than a real garden because of the restricted natural conditions. Space usually is at a premium, and this excludes the use of trees or large shrubs. Rather vines come in handy as versatile mediums to cover, to decorate or to recall the verdure of the outside world or that of the farther away countryside.

The arrangement of small shrubs and of flowers have to be considered more from the possible cultivation than from compositional points of view, these latter being developed rather according to an architectural kind of garden design. Most flowers need sun therefore; the consideration of aspect is imperative. If one side of the patio receives more of it then, the flowers will have to be planted on that side, and the other side will necessarily be greener with leafy plants or will have to receive another sort of decorative setting.

The adequate preparation of the soil and its drainage will need extra care as a sine qua non of creating proper growing conditions. In most cases though it will be more practical to cover the larger part of the patio ground with pavement rather than any kind of organic cover. If greenery is really wanted they should rather be put in raised beds or in containers than in ground level plantings. This would materially facilitate their handling, and secure their survival, with frequent waterings to make sure, and proper drainage.

A patio garden is bound to be small in extent, in elevation, and in variety as compared to an open spaced and regular sized garden. The greenery could not, and should not compete in importance with the architectural features which will be dominant and steadily present before our eyes while most of the superimposed vegetal beauties will only provide fleeting pleasures before vanishing from our view for long periods, recurring only with the rhythms of the growing seasons. And the seasonal changes, so attractive, so much inducing to change of moods in our own soul will not be as impressive and can not have as much influence as in a grassy lane of a perennial border or in a combined garden setting.

The close relation to the house, the contiguous location to it, and the organic connection with the dwelling units indoors will have to find expression in style, composition, and decoration of the patio garden. It is bound to be formal in treatment, with architectural features prevailing in the forms of steps, pavement, enclosure, furnishing, decoration, and accent.

All these with the completing additions combined into a harmonious picture will be grasped at once while looking at the patio garden from within the house as most of the time, or from the patio itself.

Potted plants in containers, vases, and other movable furnishings will create some compositional change and variety of effect by their shifted locations, but the built-in parts and erections will create the permanency of structural beauty in a patio garden.

CHAPTER IV

<u>City Garden</u>

Whoever has succeeded to create garden atmosphere
in city surroundings can live like an honorary citizen
of his own city, distinguished with decorations
without the need for investiture.

I say so.

BY THE TERM of a **city garden** we mean to
exclude suburban places which usually are less
restricted in size, in their exposure to natural effects,
and in their design requirements. City gardens are
located in more or less built-up surroundings, are
smaller in size, and are exposed to inclemencies from
environmental points of view. An observing,
adaptive, and compromising approach would bring
better and frequently the only possible good results
than sticking to an idea conceived in the abstract
without due considerations to the limiting factors
prevailing in this or that particular site.

The position of the house in relation to the area open
for garden treatment will have the dominating
influence on everything created in its proximity then,
the larger surroundings, the shape of the open area,
and the lay in relation to the sun, shades, and wind
currents.

Should you like to frequently play hide and seek with
the girl of your choice in shrubberies and thickets you
would better relinquish your honorary citizenship,

and find a country place endowed with these natural possibilities. Also, you would have to be sure about your feelings and the forms and character you are looking for in the landscape. In a city garden large shrubs, bushy surroundings and trees will probably be lacking, and your outdoor tastes will soon be detected from some of the windows in the neighbourhood to the delight of those few who like to gossip. Therefore, town gardens are especially fitting to a sedate type of city dwellers say, above the middle-aged group.

You will have to figure too that architectural features in bulk would be very costly, and if you do not win the lottery you would have to follow evening courses in masonry and carpentry then, pull up your sleeves after graduation. All these would open new opportunities for living up to your expectations and capabilities accompanied with a better appetite, stronger muscles, and rewarding self-confidence.

A garden space in the city could be on any side or on more than one side of the house but in the majority of cases it is in the rear, and corresponds to what is called a backyard, surrounded and fenced in its location. Should there be a porch or possibly a terrace at the back of the house this would enhance the setting for an overlooked design of the garden provided that the architectural surroundings of the site would properly be inducing to a formal or semiformal treatment. This is then, the typical place for a city garden.

A formal layout in classic simplicity would probably be the fitting one, but with the decorative additions you will not have to be skimpy. The close connection with the house will not only tolerate but also require more ornaments than would be the case in the same garden if located in the country. Also, irrespective of the size of the garden such compositionally built or erected features as change of levels, paths, steps, broken continuity of wall face and fence line, niches, seats and sculpture could easily create fortunate effects in the overall expression of this micro-world of its own, especially if the features would not only be telling by themselves but would be located as composing parts of the garden, or accenting terminations of lines of axes and of inner vistas.

The positioning of some of the ornaments like sculpture or water feature would have to seek a spot where sun will light them up as long as possible because light and shade will in most of the cases be given as set circumstances to which your plan will have to be adapted. The same applies to the horticultural operations with a fair chance for success. Because of these factors which are prescribed by the combined setting of each garden an asymmetrical balance will have to be worked out in most of the designs with the resulting individualities and enhanced interest in any of them.

As a contour line of elevations will less likely be present because of the lack of shrubbery and tree border, and a lack of sky space all around in the background the ground level treatment will gain in importance, especially if an overview from terrace, porch or upper story window is possible. Therefore, decorative pavement with combinative patterns would advantageously be substituted to the difficult grass or other green cover, and will prove to be a steady, unchangeable delight to the eyes. The favorite flowering plants would not have to be missed because they could freely be shifted around in pots, urns, and vases on the paved ground at will in accordance with the changing need for them.

A city garden then, will in most cases be developed as a static kind of garden to be looked at and to sit in rather than to walk around it, and to be enjoyed just as well from inside the house as from the outside.

CHAPTER V

Roof Garden

I REMEMBER from the happy times of my boyhood when climbing trees that the one who reached the top position used to announce:

> 'Én vagyok a derék legény,
> Én ülök a fa tetején'

which in free translation would sound like

> 'I am the brave guy,
> I am at the top toward the sky.'

This could also be announced by all those brave boys and girls who have succeeded to create rooftop gardens toward the sun, the winds, and the sky.

Instead of 'proceeding by elimination' the rooftop gardeners have to 'proceed by dissimulation.' There are usually some unpleasant looking adjuncts or structures on a roof top which have to be concealed first of all before any beautification of the 'grounds' can be undertaken. The next step should be to look around the outside world. Is the roof in a free position, sticking out into the space by itself or else surrounded by other stone thorns piercing into the freedom of the airspace? If you are a lonely rider you will have to protect yourself against possible weather attacks wherever they may come from but in such a clever arrangement of your defenses as not to blot out or jeopardize the possible amenities of your sky ride.

On the other hand, your defenses should also be directed toward screening out visual intrusions from Peeping Toms and Co. if neighbouring buildings would make it necessary.

Views should first be preserved, and developed by compositional means thereafter. Sun would have to be secured for a sheltered morning corner, and protecting shade for a late afternoon sitting place. Backgrounds will have to be arranged by fencing or trelliswork for the enhancement of your plant and flower effects, and accent material located for structural purposes and for aesthetic terminations. Then, and only then do you add the rest of your garden scheme, the common elements of any garden, be they sunken into the surrounding land or elevated into the realm of the birds.

Soil and water with adequate drainage would certainly have to be supplied in advance in order to create proper growing conditions, and with your water you will also strive to add that extra touch which is to become an enlivening factor of distinction. After that, you will kneel down in humble satisfaction to put down whatever paving is warranted in pattern and material of your choice, and fervently hope that the roof will hold all this even if your own weight is added to it. And if no rumbling noise from below your feet is being heard you can start announcing boldly to the world what I have quoted at the beginning of this chapter. But remember during the preceding operations to keep some of your breath for this final, triumphant chant.

After that, look out through a well placed arch or other framing toward your favorite view in the distance for a few moments of aesthetic enjoyment, and with the remainder of your physical force and will power clamber into a hammock or sit down into the comfort of a garden chair. Then, if you shut your eyes you will quietly enjoy a sense of achievement and deep contentment in your soul.

CHAPTER VI

Naturalistic Garden

"Do more bewitch me than when Art
Is too precise in every part"
                                    Herrick

"Voir dans ces champs, ces bois,
la nature affranchie,
se livrer librement a ça noble énergie."
                                    S. de Lambert

ALL THOSE people who establish themselves somewhere amidst country surroundings had many times been bewitched by Nature's charms, prospects, and mood during their earlier life. Happy childhood memories, village sojourns, river outings, hikings, campfires, summer and in the winter vacations, walks and travels are cherished deep in their souls, and these unforgettable experiences activate their yearnings, and lead them safely back into the country. There in their daily contact with the manifold manifestations of Nature's 'noble energies' they become more and more observant, sensitive, attached and content, with the lasting inner glow of a sort of quiet enthusiasm. Only the thought of their country place keeps them in emotional balance amidst the widely differing city surroundings and working conditions of their weekday lives. Because they have a place in the country.

When these people come to make an arrangement on that cherished spot of earth, to plan, to form, and to dispose the scenes of their work and play in Nature, and with Nature they are instinctively led to learn from Her the guiding principles of a **naturalistic layout**. Thereafter, much study and observation will have to be added to the store of their instinctively gathered knowledge before their gardens and grounds will bear the imprint of an **informal composition**.

With the first look on and around the place the **topography** will have to be investigated because this will have a bearing on many things. Then, the **lay** of the land in relation **to the points of** the **compass**, the direction of the prevailing **winds**, and the **sweep of the sun** in the summer and in the winter. These are of basic importance in the decision to assign the **location of the house**, followed by a functionally reasonable **circulation pattern**. Besides providing an approach and circulation the road and walk will also create the separation of **areas** which will have to be assigned to different uses. These can be shifted on paper in the planning stage until the shape, the size, and the relative location of these smaller or larger areas will correspond to the anticipated needs. Fortunately, if these use requirements will properly be taken care of their composite arrangement and appearance will very likely also satisfy the aesthetic considerations. We have to be remembered frequently that the designing of landscapes is first of all a **structural** art therefore, this division of the available land surface into separate areas is the first and foremost consideration to which all the detailed planning and decorative treatment will be added as secondaries only.

But even **before** these discoveries, investigations, and utility considerations should range the recognition of certain premises, the willing acceptance of which will happily influence all phases of gardening in the naturalistic style.

The choice of naturalistic surroundings is a clear sign of the desire to seek the freedom, mood and spaciousness of a country-like atmosphere as opposed to the restriction, mood, and confinement of a built-up neighbourhood. Once this kind of a site has successfully been secured the dominance of the **existing character** of the place has to be wholeheartedly accepted, and everything added or changed by the relatively weak hand of man should conform to that dominant natural character.

One of the basic characteristics of natural surroundings is **reposefulness**, and this should by all means be retained as a most desirable attribute of a naturalistic garden. Great help in achieving this reposefulness will be given by striving to **simplicity** in the arrangement, and in the materials used in the arrangement. A few bold strokes will prove more successful than any pottering with puny details. The use of **masses** rather than that of singles or smaller units, **uncluttered open spaces** rather than scatterings should be the rule. **Quiet, blending hues** rather than jarring tones will mould harmoniously into nature's unostentatiously green habitation. And the skillful planning of the shifting **light and shade effects** as well as the induced serenity of properly chosen or composed **perspectives** will also greatly contribute to naturalistic repose.

The **redisposition** of human tendencies will also be needed, form skimpiness to generosity, from

31

compressed to expansive, from man-sized to nature-sized, and from the precious little to liberal profusion.

We may add the detachment form accustomed straight lines and 90° angles, and our application of William Hogarth's famous **undulating line**, the 'Line of Beauty' since 1745, or from much earlier times indeed, to the outlines of our naturalistic creations.

Special attention will be needed to the **verticals**, which will provide the frame and enclosure of the garden, the contours of the skyline, the directing elements of the vistas, and the all-important flanking masses to the perspectives. This point will lead to a careful study, and attentive treatment of the **foreground**.

Natural grounds have in almost every location some kind of **individuality** in their lay or in some of their features. These should be recognized and seized upon from the outset, and throughout the developing process. Any addition to the ground, any planting on it should not counteract, and this way neutralize these felicitous occurrences or weaken their effect but rather play upon, point up, and intensify the characteristics expressed in them. As the years go by, trees and shrubs grow, plants multiply, and the ground is becoming more and more subdued under their dominance. Try to keep in mind and in your favour those characteristic features of your original recognition and emphasis, preserve their special status, and secure thereby the enduring individual harmony and unity of your naturalistic garden picture.

A careful observance of the directions of all these guideposts will secure the **pictorial quality** of a naturalistic composition, which should be the chief aim besides or rather with the usefulness of the layout.

Then, when it comes to the **working out of details** we should pay heed to the advice of that wise and sympathetic American gardener of 1889, William McMillan who advocated the "softening what is hard, clothing what is bare, filling out what is meager and enriching what is beautiful, all in harmony with the original type" in a landscape garden.

There are different kinds of naturalistic gardens some of which will be treated in the following chapters. These lay stress, and work upon some distinctive feature as the main theme of their composition but due attention to the enumerated general principles will lead to their good design, and to their artistic layout.

Naturalistic gardening has a pleasantly insinuating, and successively pervasive influence upon human minds and emotions. In due course, this immaterial acting power is turned back into the garden in the form of continuous improvement, changes, additions, deletions, and perfections with the observing ability and attentive care of a landscape painter, with the warmhearted dealing of a lover. These positive emotions coupled with active planning and tending is bound to grow as years follow years, and the insinuative suggestions never cease, rather grow in potency. From the death-bed will still plans and advises be forthcoming to favour the naturalistic garden, and as its master is being lowered into the grave the vivacity of his last thoughts to still unfinished tasks will bring him back to life. Believe me, dear friends, it pays to have established close connections, and to be in good terms with major natural forces.

That accomplished and famous English landscape gardener, Humphrey Repton has properly expressed the reactive effect of human dealings with the materials, features, and scenes of the landscape in these words: "Landscape gardening is, if possible, to inculcate the great secret of true happiness."

CHAPTER VII

Bog Gardening

"Where the heron, the Shuh-shuh-gah,
Feeds among the reeds and rushes."
Longfellow

TALKING of bogs and swamps you have to shed your instinctive fears. Disassociate your mind from malaria-breeding grounds, from yellow fever, and from oppressing nightmares. Highwaymen do not hide any more in bogs, marshes, and swampy land because there is no comfort there for counting their spoil, and the campfire of their haunt could easily be detected by air-patrols from above. Therefore, they rather flee from the shame of their misdeed with speedy Cadillacs into luxurious motels recommended by tourist associations, and there from easy chairs follow on television the announcements about their robbery. Neither do bogeymen choose these places for their sporting grounds. And the bubbling you may notice sometimes, is not coming from the whiffs and puffs of hidden witches, but is the signs of escaping marsh gases.

True enough, frogs, snakes, and other creatures may have discovered before you how attractive and pleasant such places can be, and have multiplied undisturbed by human interference, but they are harmless in most instances, and will do quite good services to the bog or swamp garden. Besides, as you proceed with your added plantings the proportionate number of frogs and water snakes will lessen as the flowers and other bog plants will spread far and wide. So, just do not worry.

The chief characteristic of a bog is the accumulation of peat in different compositions and in different stages of decomposition of the water-loving plants, which constitute it, sphagnum moss being an important part of it. Sphagnum moss most often has a simultaneous life and death stage, thriving at the top in a green, soft, cushiony layer, and decaying in pale coloured layers below it, above the many layers of decomposed plant residues underneath in so many feet thickness. To walk upon this accumulation of organic matter is springy as the steps sink into the soft substance. But it is not considerate to walk frequently on this wonderful stuff, rather plant in them those flowers which revel in this kind of places like pitcher plants, hardy orchids, Venus's flytrap, and other insect-catching plants, or in a swampy place the purple loosestrife, cardinal flower, fringed gentian, turtle head, bee balm, and the rest, in masses.

What regards mosquitoes around here they are harmless 'skeeters' whose nickname in Latin is **Culex**, while the malaria breeders are the **Anopheles** kind which even sounds more serious. Should you not believe this you could watch them when seated because the 'skeeters' hold themselves parallel to the surface, and the malaria breeder type, when at rest, are poised at a 45° angle. So, when not at rest but buzzing around you may want to run. It is good news though that your fears could be alleviated right away by 50% in knowing that their stronger sex is content to browse only in the grass and weeds, and only the females do the biting, only they are the villains who go for blood. It has to be admitted that I have never come to find out if the Anopheles practice monogamy, and are in equal numbers, or keep several wives maybe for their amenity of blood content, and thereby destroying the balance of risk.

I am also wondering what happens if the females become mad and dissatisfied with the males for some reason, do they keep their poised attitude even then? And how can you know, if you are really worried, if **he** is going to browse, or **she** is coming to bite? And after all, how do you know which one is a male or female, especially when they are in flight toward your neck or shoulder, and are not at rest, poised at a 45° angle? One thing you can do is to put up your glasses, and watch their legs. Those are the females that wear mini-skirts.

If you do not want to take chances with the females just as well as with humans you may greatly be relieved by the realization that the mosquitoes of the feminine sex are actively engaged only at night. Once this is revealed, you will be encouraged to lead a decently sober life which would also benefit your bog-gardening activities.

As a matter of fact, if you have a boggy or swampy place most of their characteristic native plants are likely to be there, and your task will greatly be simplified. You certainly will refrain from filling or draining that genuinely beautiful piece of ground. The main thing to do then, is to arrange the surroundings and approaches in such a way that they serve their purpose and please the eye from a structural point of view.

Should you try to approximate because you cannot entirely imitate the necessary conditions of a bog or swamp within your limited garden space you may try your hand at it with a depression or low lying clayey ground with lighter soil added to it, or with raised beds where continually moist conditions couple with good drainage can be secured. Also, you may spread some moss on the wet ground to prevent the mud from spoiling the clean appearance of the beautiful foliage of your plantings. This will also serve to keep the soil in the required moist condition.

If you have succeeded to create the necessary conditions for growing the plants that like a boggy or swampy habitat then, you will want to have hardy orchids, insectivorous plants such as butterwort, sundew, and the already mentioned pitcher plants and Venus" flytrap then, primulas, sneezeweed, arrowhead, marsh marigolds, forget-me-nots, marshmallows, purple loosestrife, and Lilium superbum or Lilium Canadense. Irises would certainly thrive there as well as sedges, rushes, decorative grasses, and ferns.

Should you have a larger place you surely would want the effect of height introduced. Shrubs like swamp honeysuckle, white azalea, sheep laurel, black alder, wild rosemary, mountain holly, willows, button-bush, winter-berry, deer-berry, creeping snowberry, and more of their kind could find a place there, with suitable trees like white cedar, spruce and tamarack judiciously grouped among them.

By the time you will have added the swamp milkweed, swamp rose and swamp loosestrife then, the bog bean, bog shinleaf and bog pimpernel you will be swamped with foliage and flowers, and bogged down in your bog to have at least become yourself a boggy man or boggy woman.

CHAPTER VIII

Rock Gardens

"Johnson's style was grand and Gibson's elegant ....
Johnson hewed passages through the Alps, while
Gibson leveled walks through parks and gardens."
George Colman

'LET the little children ... coming unto me,' said the
Lord, and so does many a gardener when thinking of
his garden flock.

There is a special kind of attractiveness in smallness
which brings the smiles on the face and in the soul of
the mighty who enjoy the pleasant company of little
ones. Especially so if these show such a sincere
brightness as the alpines. Those giants of the 'homo
sapiens' who are touched by their special charms will
kneel down to enjoy the beauty of these little gems
from near view, spontaneously expressing thereby the
intensity of their feelings. And the little flowers will
sparkle with brilliancy, but not out of showiness or
frivolity but out of childish exuberance. They seem
to strengthen the likelihood of the good-humored
Alpine saying 'Da oben auf der Alm Da gibt's ka
Sünd,' here on high pastureland there is no sin.

These innocent little flowers of the pure mountain
airs have come from the climatic hardships of high,
exposed altitudes, but again the barometric pressure
has increased and weighs on them by the very fact of
their descent. Therefore, it is only rational to show

kindness to them. This means to create all the required special conditions, which are needed to their well being, and also to secure the cherished prospects of mountain scenery, the peaks and valleys, rocks and ravines lest they become homesick. In addition to our human associations with mountain experiences this is then, part of the underlying psychology of rock gardening.

To better understand the physiology of these plants from high mountains we may think of some of the many peculiarities, which are associated with their existence.

The soil is generally warmer up there than the air which being rarified cannot absorb much solar rays. The flowers in these exposed situations therefore, stay little or bend down in order to cling quite close to the soil. True, there is quite a difference in the soil temperature during the day and night conditions, but the above-ground parts of the plants are well equipped for the icy nights while their long roots in the depth enjoy more equalized temperature. The strange and seemingly incongruous companionship of the fragile little flowers and the solid rocks and boulders is also better understandable by knowing that the rocks absorb much heat during the day, and by giving it off at night prevent a sudden temperature change in their proximity. This way they shelter their little friends who seek their protection, and cluster around them happily.

The brilliancy of their colours is due to the abundance of ultra-violet rays on high altitudes. I wonder how or rather how long and to what extent can these flowers of our rock gardens retain their brilliancy, as those rays are absorbed to a larger degree by the denser atmosphere of lower-lying grounds?

They are used to and need much humidity because at any high altitude they had much atmospheric humidity, and also heavy dew on the ground. At the same time, drainage conditions up there are very good; consequently, these flowers do not suffer water for long on their crowns.

The herbaceous perennials coming from high above have had different dwelling places in the mountains, and accordingly have been adapted to different life conditions. Some have been brought up in forest clearings, some much less numerous ones in the humid shade of dense forest growth. Others were gaily spread in masses of colour on the mountain meadows giving thereby to these places their fairy enchantment in the frame of the spectacular scenery of peaks and crest. Some others again have attained their speedy development on the floor of brighter deciduous forests before the leafage of the trees would interfere and bar them from the much needed sunshine and light. Some have preferred the soft grassy comfort in the sun, some the deep fissures or smaller crevices of rock groupings, and some others the trickling water of a miniature source.

All these preferences, and well-established life habits and requirements, and many more of them would have to be considered when arranging for their transferred habitation in the rock garden. Their thriving happiness in their restricted new living quarters and soil pockets as well as the success of the gardener's tending care will depend on trying to imitate as closely as possible the aggregate conditions of the original habitat of these high-bred plants and flowers.

Annuals are only a few compared to the perennial vegetation of high mountain districts. This is easily understandable considering the shortness of the season during which their lifecycle has to be accomplished. Then, the frequent inclemencies occurring during their growing seasons is likely to cut into their reproductive capacity, into the very continuity of their precarious existence because they cannot reach the stage of seed formation.

Dwarf, compact growing shrubs would not only give **variety** in their size, shape, and colour as contrasted with the flowers but would also be useful to create the partitioning of such a motley gathering as the many kinds of alpines present when crammed into a small area of our rock gardens. Tiny layouts, with due regard to proportions would only have the space for the truly miniature kind of shrubs.

Cooling of the rock garden atmosphere is of especial importance in the North American climate of hot and dry summers in which the heated period of the days is long. The home atmosphere of these mountain flowers is humid which is due to several climatic causes. And the drainage of the uplands is well secured by their geologic formations and their soil compositions.

This good **drainage** too is of great importance, and should be provided for the rock garden tenants. They need almost constant water supply and well-cooled conditions to their many roots and rootlets as well as to their immediate atmosphere above ground. Both can easier be secured by sinking the position of the rock garden, and by introducing an adequate water supply on such sites where these are practicable.

The rock garden is a feature apart, separate not only from its location point of view but also from some points of the aesthetics which generally govern the arrangement of other features in the garden scene. For example, no repetitions are advisable because no creation of rhythm is to be planned in the limited space where a motley multitude of different shapes and colours are brought together. No balance either, neither the symmetrical nor the asymmetrical type, as this latter is used in naturalistic layout. The rock garden is a picturesque feature with much broken ground, small depressions, and large or larger rocks visible in bold, impressive groupings, and some startling climaxes built irregularly on turning points or elevations, which are to be pointed up or emphasized.

There are no straight lines or geometrical forms worked into the layout, as the smoothly flowing curves of the landscape style will also be absent. The forms of the detached small planting areas, and also the lines of the paths will be irregular in their lay, shape, and size, or else in their width and direction, with sudden, sharp turns as the protruding rock masses would necessitate them. We cannot talk of a determinable aspect either because within the rock garden will be countless variances with diversified exposures. Neither could we speak of a layout whose regular features would give at once a clear understanding of what is meant to be conveyed to the spectator by the design, nor of an informal design to reveal itself in well developed stages, and to be sensed by moving about in an intended and skillfully arranged sequence.

"The most desirable type of rock garden is that which is made on a spot where rocks are found ... With few additions of rocks and proper preparation of the soil all that you then require is the plant material ... Before you move a rock take a few days off to study rocky hillsides and the nature of the rocks in your locality – see what kind of stone it is and how the stones lie in the soil. In most instances you will discover that the stones are imbedded in fairly comfortable looking positions as though they had settled down to enjoy themselves ..." *

As I am living in the North I can only encourage everybody to plant many, many Crocuses and possibly Soldanellas in order to let them melt and pierce the snow at so many places and so many times that it should give up its hold soon, and rather leave crying with tears.

* The Practical Book of Outdoor Flowers, by Richardson Wright. Garden City Publishing Company, Inc., Garden City, New York, 1924, copyright J. B. Lippincott Company

CHAPTER IX

Wall Garden

" …look at these airy lines of relationship
whose balance marks strength in long
endurable lines."
Ann Born: Dry stone walls

THE MYSTERIOUS hand could not have written
the fateful Mene, Mene, Tekel, Upharsin on the wall
would this had been laid dry* with rock plants in the
crevices. The tufts, rosettes, and carpeting of the
alpine flowers would have thwarted the foreboding,
Belshazzar's feast could have continued undisturbed,
and the fall of Babylon might have been avoided.
Nor would the wall of Jericho have fallen before
Joshua would they not have been conventionally built
because the beauty of a planted wall might have saved
them from destruction.

These are merely conjectures, and may sound a bit
far-fetched. True it is the fact though that planted
walls can be such beautiful additions to the garden
scene that they arrest the gaze and the walking steps
by their peculiar attractions. They belong to a class of
their own as a feature all together apart in their
combination although the composing rocks and
plants can also be used separately or together in other
ways.

* Note: The so-called **dry wall** is built without mortar or cement.

45

Before any wall is constructed their fitness from compositional points of view in the garden should carefully be considered. Their bulk, vertical stand, conspicuousness, disparate texture, and strongly accented line in the garden picture cannot be treated as a separate entity irrespective of its surroundings but has to be composed as an integral part and important parcel of the whole layout. Also, irrespective of its decorative qualities and pleasing aspect the more functional roles the wall can fulfill the more will it prove its value.

Should it prove its worth as a separation and holder of levels, as a divisional element between garden areas, as a protection against wind or bodily and visual intrusions, as a screen, enclosing frame or termination of space and effect, and possibly embodying several of these tasks at the same time the more will it gain stature among the less versatile structural elements of the garden. Add to these services the esthetical value it represents in itself if attractively built, and by its floral host of charming little plants, and their combinative impression then, its secondary services as for instance the backing it provides to plantings put in their front or in the line of vision leading toward them, serving as a seat if built to sitting height, or carrying a balustrade, urns, pots or vases, and you will surely exert your planning faculties to make out of your planted dry wall a real success.

Although walls can be built of bricks or other materials too the most attractive ones are of stones, especially if they attain a certain height. Brick is useful for low walls, built dry, and adapted to many uses and situations even in the smallest garden. Their use had to be influenced by the type of garden they are put in, in order to be congruous with their setting.

When it comes to using stones which are especially fortunate additions to any naturalistic place it is worth while to spend some time on the characteristics of the kind of stones to be chosen. In case they occur naturally on the spot their geologic formation as a rule is vouching for their fitness to their surroundings. They should not only be of blending colour and texture but also resistant to the decomposing effects of freezing, and the alternation of freezing and thawing so characteristic to the northeast American climate. They would not be good for dry walling if adversely affected and crumbling under these climatic influences. Whether they should be limestone, sandstone or granite is largely a matter of the local or nearby quarrying possibilities in the case of most garden builders. Their size and form is another matter.

The size of stones as a building material seems to have changed in an adverse ratio with the advance of civilization. The ancient Egyptians in Africa, the Incas in South America, and the Romans in their far-spread empire have used large chunks of stone for their architecture in different structural and decorative ways, but the late twentieth century man does not want to lift a stone if larger than an ostrich egg. In the latter case he flees the spot of his find, soon to return riding high on some kind of heavy machinery, and to push everything aside of its way, and bury under. From purely esthetical point of view this is a pity because large pieces of stone put together for some purposes in natural surroundings are more suitable, fit much better, and look nicer than small or pebble-sized ones. Applied to dry walling the size of the stones used should bear proper relation to the height of the wall, larger stones being more appropriate to higher walls than to the lower ones.

Large pieces with their weight are also more useful to hold the earth they are supposed to retain, and to withstand the hydaulic pressure exerted on them form the soil behind.

As to their form, stones more or less angular and of flattish shape rather be chosen with sufficient width so as not to produce too many layers when built, one row called course upon the other. Round stones are not so satisfactory for the purpose, but the irregularity of untrimmed natural stones would prove an advantage from the points of laying them, and planting them.

Proper foundation is a must in most northeastern regions because of the deep penetration of frost into the soil, and the heaving and dislocating effect of the expanding surface soil due to the frequently occurring alternate freezing and thawing.

Should the change of level be pretty high one high wallface could not properly be built, and should be divided into two or more lower walls with a strip of land and a bank in between them. This partitioning would not only be safer from a structural point of view but would also lessen the apparent height of the change of levels, and aesthetically be more pleasing.

When we consider the advantage of wallfaces for planting purposes we may note the small space required in comparison to the flower beds laid flat on the ground. This is the same use of the airspace on a smaller scale than what the skyscrapers are built for on restricted city grounds. Then, many plants could not live on a level surface, especially in heavy clay which is retentive of moisture, and waterlogged in winter, but they can make their home and thrive in their vertical position where they can get an unfailing supply of moisture under well-drained conditions.

The customary subjects for wall gardening are the dwarf **alpines**, and all the so-called **rock plants**. Those with drooping or trailing habit are especially fitting and beautiful. All these require some work to keep them and the overall view of the wall in proper shape. Therefore, it seems that the vegetal beautification of wall spaces could just as well be achieved with such **vines** and **trailing shrubs** that produce beautiful flowers, leaves, and berries in variety and easy profusion because they are native or well adapted to our climate. These plants once established at the top, and some at the bottom of the wall require little in after-care, and delight us all through the seasons with beautifully textured and diversified foliage on mostly pendulous branches.

CHAPTER X

Water Garden

"Come away, O human child!
To the waters and the wild …
With a faery, hand in hand
For the world's more full of weeping
than you can understand."

Yeats

"To those who have believed and wrought the works of righteousness the good tidings that for them are Gardens through which the rivers flow… and therein will they abide."

The Koran

"Allah a prépare pour ceux qui croient en lui des jardins sous lesquels coulent les ruisseaux; ils y demeureront toujours: c'est la plus grand félicite."

Le Coran

ENHANCE that promised felicity with plantings in that brook or lake, pool or pond, and around the margins or on the banks. The setting is just perfect for developing further their inherent beauty that has universal appeal to the human soul. The waterside is sure to attract young and old alike, and while the former would stealingly approach the frogs, and throw stones in the water, the latter may enjoy the varied beauty of the plants, and the rippling of the water surface.

Anyone can have the pleasure of growing **water lilies** in some part of his garden or yard if he makes a relatively small or larger hole in the ground for them where he can sink some container, put rich soil and keep water in it there to cultivate some hardy Nymphaeas, and maybe Nelumbiums. The position should be chosen in a sunny and airy spot with no overhanging trees. Once this courageous step has been made, the lush green leaves will spread on the water, and among them the beautiful large flowers will open and bloom with remarkable persistency. A few fish and possibly frogs, and the plants themselves will create the necessary balanced aquatic conditions so that the water stays clear, and the plants keep healthy.

In completion of this garden feature so pleasingly different in material, mood and effect you will create a kind of **surrounding plantation** which would be in keeping with the character of the lily pool like ornamental grasses and sedges or irises.

Although the presence of water, and water-loving plants will improve any garden surrounding the **form of** the **pool** will have a bearing on the overall beauty of the garden picture, and will have to conform in outline and proportions to the rest of the composition so as to be a fitting and completing structural element, and not one which disturbs the compositional harmony, and detracts form its balanced unity.

If the pool is to be in a **formal** layout the principals of the formation of formal gardens will have to be complied with. Most likely but not necessarily the pool will occupy a central position because of its conspicuous and composite beauty, and because the overall flatness of its appearance would not interfere with the unbroken continuity of the axis line in a longitudinal axis arrangement. Still, a lower type of decoration in the pool, be it sculptural or some other kind could quite fittingly be used. On the other hand, in a central-motive formal garden where the accent is centered and all the other structural lines and approaches lead up to that point a pool with some beautiful standing fountain, prominent sculpture or sculptural group in the middle would be a most fortunately created climax in the composition.

The lily pool could just as well be at the crossing points of paths or at the termination of one of them with a bench on the other side for the quiet enjoyment of the nymphaeas, with trees and shrubs forming the background, and providing reflections in the intermittent open surface of the water.

The coping of all these artificial pools should be set around the edges on a restrained way rather than prominently, with the exception of the fitting occasions for central-motive applications.

In an **informal** arrangement which is frequently being found in the more or less restricted places of suburban or even city gardens the topography of the site, and a fitting choice for the location of the pool should lead the designer, but he will have more playroom for his imaginative planning. The plants to grow will be the same, but he will have more freedom to plant several types of aquatics and marginal plants, and also to use them more profusely than in a formal settings would be possible for him. Naturally, this more liberal treatment also depends on the size of the place, and on the proportional requirements.

In **all cases** of water lily plantings restraint in the number of plants used will crate more happy results than over-plantings. Like with the use of vines on wall faces where more beauty will be achieved with partial coverings, and open wall spaces left for showing the beauties peculiar to them instead of smothering the walls and all parts of the buildings with greenery. Likewise, the partially open water surfaces will show brightly gleaming patches amidst the greenery, and will reflect the lights of the day and of the night, adding thereby the peculiar beauty of water to the picture in the pleasing variety of a distinct substance, surface, colours, reflections, and placidity.

When we go out of town or suburbs the grounds of the wider **countryside** offer many opportunities to mind and muscles. There are always undulations on the ground, declivities with dips at their bottom, brooks, ditches, ravines, and rivulets, ponds and lakes. All these places could easily be converted to water gardening with felicitous results. Should they have more or less stagnant water, slow moving flow or swifter current the plants to be grown in them would have to be judiciously selected in accordance with their preferred water habitat, and the given circumstances of the climate, soil, aspects, and exposures.

A **pond** would require a quiet and reposeful treatment, with flower-studded grass reaching down to the water's edge, with taller herbaceous plants in the shelter of coves, and accented plantations on the promontories. The massive shapes of a few boulders or rocks on the banks and in the shallow water will happily enhance the fragile beauty of the marginal flowers, and of the slender, pliant forms of the reeds and rushes. The reflections would have more scope to intensify, vary, and make more striking the manifold beauties of texture, form, and colour of the surrounding vegetation.

Should there be a **brook** or **rivulet** crossing or adjoining the site this would give a continuous water supply with constantly moist conditions on the edges, and also in the further reaches by way of capillarity. This enables the gardener to grow an ample variety of beautiful plants from the tiny Forget-me-nots to the Royal Ferns, and the huge leaved Gunnera in England or the ornamental rhubarbs in America.

The **waterside shrubs** and **trees** will lend their charms to the happy scene. Pendulous willows will spread their branches over the water and the waterside, dipping a branchlet here and there into the current. Birches, Alders, Swamp Maples and Ashes will share each other's company in thriving, contented opulence, and lend their aesthetic assistance to a composite waterside picture. How appropriately and beautifully has expressed Delisle this mutuality of tree and water-current,

"… L'arbre et les eaux se prêtent leurs secours:
L'onde rajeunit l'arbre, et l'arbre orne son cours"

CHAPTER XI

Wild Gardening

"The basis of any wild garden must be the idealization of some natural habitat. It matters little what the habitat may be, so long as its typical pattern is accentuated, organized into a composition and given its appropriate setting."
Sylvia Crowe

HERE WE ARE, our old friends, Louise and Nellie together with George and Richard who are back again.

"Hallo, Nellie, I have big news for you. We have bought a place in the country. It is as wild as the Sierra Nevada, and it is our turn now to make a garden there. I have seen the place yesterday, and I am wondering, I should even say I am concerned of how could I make use of what I have learnt from you in the art of laying out a garden."

"Well, that is secondary, Louise, the main thing is that you have got a place. Congratulations to both of you."

"Thanks, Nellie, but the chief instigator has really been George, and he has committed the whole purchase in a sudden whiff of furor. Now, he is in an entirely changed mood, and seems to be genuinely pleased with the deal. His face is frequently lit up with smiles, and he is grinning occasionally. He also laughed in his sleep a few times. I am slightly worried, Nellie."

"Oh my! You don't have to, Louise, I think these are sure signs that he is satisfied with what he has done. But tell me how has the whole thing come about?"

"You know, Nellie, since we have visited your beautiful place I have several times talked about formal gardens to George, and have explained some of those designing principals you have explained to me. He has kept silent most of the time though, and sometimes has moved his head with a kind of negative jerk. Then, the day before yesterday when I have brought up the subject again he hasn't said anything to it but has sunken into a sullen mood, and his face has gradually become reddish. As we have had no beefsteak for quite a while because of the cost, and I have also hidden from him the whiskey I have concluded that he has not liked what I was talking about. He seemed to have used his self-control for which Englishmen are so famous although his temper has gradually and visibly mounted. I have instinctively stopped talking about formality; and he has regained his composure. Later, he has started talking at last, and has brought up a few points about the Anglo-Saxons. When, at last, he has referred to Herrick, and has talked about such things as 'erring sweetness' it has occurred to me that possibly both of us would have better chances in a country place where no formalities prevail."

"I see that. But say it to me, Louise, what do you intend to do with the whiskey you have hidden from George?"

"I am going to drink it myself."

"Times and morals are changing, Nellie. We have spent those years away from home, and you pick up things as you go along, you know."

"My! This is a second surprise to me. Would it not be preposterous from me to ask you to leave some in the bottle for our common celebration of you new departure in life, I mean for your wild gardening?"

"Sure, sure, don't worry, we will have that together for sure."

"Good news. And as you have mentioned about 'erring sweetness' would it be possible for me to join you on some weekends in the wild?"

"All right, Nellie, but I have to remind you beforehand of two important contributions to good results in naturalistic gardening namely, to **surprise** and **discovery** if you properly understand what I mean. And, I suppose you will come together with Richard won't you?"

"That is understood, do not worry about that. Ha ha! I would feel lost by myself in the Sierra. But tell me further about your purchase."

"Well, while expounding **his** ideas about gardening, and the strong Teutonic strains in our racial characteristics it was my turn to keep silent and listen attentively to his talk. Suddenly, George looked at me with a kind of sharp scrutiny in his eyes. 'And you too should show at last some appreciation of what I am saying to you all the time.' At that point I have jumped onto his neck, and have stayed there for a while. When later, George got up he left hurriedly, and drove away. When I have seen him again yesterday, he has become a changed man. Then, again he ran away, and is just back from the woods. He is in a talkative mood about his plans, some of them grandiose indeed. So, from now on, both of us will have to adjust ourselves to our changed conditions, and also to the changes in our budget for about ten years. **This** is then, the true story, Nellie, how we have gone wild."

"My! This is really something, isn't it?"

"Yes, Nellie. And another thing is, for contrast's sake, that I am pretty sure to have a tame little child in about nine months' time."

"Louise! This is the third big surprise for me. The whole thing is absolutely fantastic. I have to tell it to Richard who is just here. Wait."

It has taken some time for Nellie, joined by Louise, to fight off then, to wipe off their tears before their discussion could continue.

"All further information, Nellie, would have to come from George who has come to the 'phone, and stands beside me in all his naturalistic but not at all wild looking grandeur."

"Hallo, Nellie, how are you?"

"Fine, thanks George, and much surprised. Congratulations for your feat."

"Which one, Nellie?"

"O, George, don't make fun out of it. Rather tell me about your new undertaking, and the plan you have with you Sierra."

"I haven't got a plan as you would think of it, Nellie, in a coherent and tightly organized way. I am rather full of plans, and I would not know for the time being with which one to begin. I am running around the place, and up and down 'comme un petit fou' and see countless opportunities at every corner for wild gardening.

There is a real wood at the place with standing timber, another small one with different kinds of young growth in it, a halfway open hill with a small dip in the middle, and a large hollow running down all along the side of the hill. There are outcroppings close to the top of the hill, a large perpendicular rock face at the high end of the hollow, and scattered rocks all over the place including the grassy parcel of land down on the level part wherefrom the entrance road will have to be built."

"This sounds really exciting doesn't it?"

"Yes, I am excited, and find it hard to fall asleep at night because of my changing plans in my thoughts. Louise says that I behave funny while asleep but I wouldn't know about that. What I do know is that I shall start working at some of my plans right away in order to take the rest of them off my mind. I shall disappear from civilized society for awhile with a few sandwiches, donuts, and apples in my bag, and a few bottles which I am going to cool in somewhere in a water-hole, or hide under the fallen leaves."

"Will those be whiskey bottles, George, or some other spirits?"

"O no! That would not be in the spirit of natural surroundings where a balanced reasonableness, a sober mood, and quiet harmony prevail. But possibly some beer, I have to admit that, which would taste good after the physical labour of a working day. But this is just by the way, and contributory only to the plans I have, and which I shall try to convey to you by describing the grounds as if we would be proceeding together from end to end."

I'll make good company to you, George, and I shall be listening."

"Well, to begin right at the new start, I have seen a nice spot where the hill meets the level which after cutting into the hill on the higher part should be cleared from the small trees and other growth, and be made for a playground because we will soon have a little boy to run around as Louise has told you."

"Do you know about it too, George? I have thought it to be a secret between girl friends only."

"I am only guessing after what I have overheard from Louise's declaration to you, Nellie."

"I see. Please continue."

"At that spot no flowers will be grown, not even wild ones. But just below that spot there is a similar place with scattered growth only. There the existing vegetation with all the tough roots would have to be pushed aside to make place for vegetable patches close to a future dwelling, and for flower plots toward the entrance part of the grounds. Between them a wide path would run from the separation line and some small fruit bushes for screening and other good purposes. Both areas, the playground, and the vegetable-flower garden could be viewed and supervised form the windows.

From this latter described place a kind of grassy lane leads among bushes toward the small wood of varied younger growth. A half-ready path-like opening to the left leads into this where a few thinnings would make the path continuous, and would provide semi-shade or dappled shade along its course. An ideal place for quite a few wild flowers, bulbs, and ferns which thrive in this kind of atmosphere. And under the trees some other kinds will feel at home.

All this little wood is quite close to the spot where I intend to locate the cottage or cabin. Therefore, to the Southwest of that location a path of the mainly shrubby growth will have to be cleared to make room for some brighter, sunnier spot for such flowers, encircled by flowering bushes which like the sunny exposure, and endure the heat of our dry summers.

Proceeding from this patch of wood the ground rises. We walk up sideways to the wooded hill. Here a rough stone step with one or two landings would be most fitting with rock plants in the crevices, and a wealth of annuals maybe on both sides because this side has the same sunny, southwestern exposure than the small wood below.

Turning into the wood to the left we get into real dense forest of mainly spruces. Here some cleared recesses with adequate plantings would add variety to the monotony of serried racks of conifers, and some long depressions in the forest floor would easily lend themselves to be developed into beautiful glades.

The path across this wooded hill should be left in its natural state with almost no leveling, and the needleleaf covering would be preserved. Shade-loving wild flowers and bushes would spread irregularly away from this path among the trees with occasional vines to climb around and up the chosen trunks of trees.

The highest point in the woods happens to be just in the middle of it where rocks form a semi-circle and where also larger trees stand the dry lower branches of which will have to be cut off. At this central spot wherefrom a descending path will lead toward the other end of the woods a kind of forest rest will be arranged with seats in front of the rocks, and some sawn pieces of tree trunks for using them as small rustic tables. If a source could somehow be found to serve this spot with water that would be a most welcome addition and improvement indeed for both plants and humans.

As we follow the outgoing paths there are some breaks among the trees, and some more clearings would have to be made in order to get glimpses of the countryside below, and the distant landscape beyond. As these breaks will be short ones because the edge of the wood is nearby they will not have to be wide, and the shining midday and afternoon sun will accentuate our views into the open country. Also, we will have good chances to framing our views towards selected parts of the landscape.

On half-shady spots along the outgoing path as well as on the edges of the wood both inside and outside some broad-leaf evergreen shrubs would make a beautiful show when in flower, and also when in their green attire. For planting on the outskirts of the forest quite a choice of small flowering trees and large flowering bushes would be available, all of them desirable subjects. In front of them some of the rank-growing hardy native wild flowers would colour the hillside in late summer and in the fall."

"George, please."

"The half-open hillside would provide many aspects and situations to turn the whole into a beauty spot, and where the rock outcroppings are there a perfect rock garden could be created."

"George please."

"Just below the rocks there is a beautiful small pine grove, and from there the prospect all around is most beautiful. The hollow part along the hillside seems to just have been created and offer ample opportunities for wild gardening, and if some watercourse could be led into it you wouldn't like to leave the spot. Everything the space on the very grounds offer could be included in wild gardening by slow growth, and with no hurry, Nellie."

"Geooorge, Geooorge, pleeease!"
"What?"

"I am just speechless after hearing your spirited account, George. Many, many thanks for it."

"You know, Nellie, frankly speaking, I have faith in that land."

"No wonder, George, you have always shown signs of paganism, wild man. But would you call Louise for just a moment please because I have to rush now, and leave in a hurry."

"Yes, Nellie, and thank you for your interest."

"Hallo, dear!"

"I am so happy, Louise that you and George are on the right way to achieve something so congenial and exciting which surpasses my wildest dreams. I may even ask you to let me be buried, when it becomes necessary, under that pine grove, in front of the rock outcroppings on the hillside. But right now, I have to hurry, Louise because a sale will just start at the Stork Store, and I want to buy a few clothes."

"At the Stork Store? For my baby?"

"No, for mine, Louise, in about eight month's time."

"Mmyy! Everything has got so wild around here suddenly. I'll meet you there, Nellie. By' now!"

Note. Richard got only a minor role to play in the happenings.

GARDENS GALORE;

An Epilogue

ELEVEN TYPES of gardens have been treated, but our craving for their kind has not been saturated for that. The **genus gardenicus** has many species, and many more varieties.

Children's gardens, bird gardens, and botanical gardens; school gardens, experimental gardens, and hanging gardens; spring gardens, night gardens, and fragrant gardens for the blind; iris gardens, herb gardens, and weed or weedy gardens; cottage gardens full with flowers, and lovers' gardens full with associations; sit-out and walking gardens for recovery homes, and jumping gardens for those of grasshopper age; gardens for tropical or for temperate conditions and beer-gardens for the intemperate ones; gardens for medicinal plants then, memorial gardens.

The list has not been exhausted though by arriving into Pine Crest Cemetery because the neighbouring municipal park has been designed and arranged for the more active types than those resting in their neighbourhood. Garden allotments, garden suburbs, garden towns, and garden villages, have been devised and created, parkways built and green-belts established, but frankly, I would be going further than that.

I would suggest garden-rings around the globe that could follow the latitudes, and also the longitudes for more variety's sake. Then the **gardener emeritus** like a kind of yogi should be freed from his very earthly chores, and have the privilege of walking or be pushed around these lines to enjoy gardens after gardens, to compare, to observe, and to freely criticize, to teach and to learn, and to leisurely exchange his views with those ladies and gentlemen engaged in the same kind of pilgrimage. Also to gather seeds and seedlings but no cuttings or divisions would be allowed. The gathering of flowers should be free though because these seasoned gardeners could be trusted to use their qualified judgment in these matters. And also to gather the necessaries for their upkeep from the vegetable patches. Hunting would not be allowed for security reasons, and the policing could be done by the keepers but tipping would strictly be prohibited.

Island hopping in groups would be arranged for those seeking seashores, or else they could take a loop, and return by another meridian. Financing for this detached way of life would mainly be coming from the retirement benefits, and for those gardeners of less developed areas from the special allocations assessed and distributed by the World Ring Garden Club with no outsiders holding office in it, only such gardeners who for some serious reason could not make the rings.

This is then, the grand project that would make it even more alluring to grow into garden retirement. There would be no separating garden curtain, only the easily penetrable divisional hedgerows and shrubberies, and the free exchange of gardening ideas and materials could contribute to fertilize our humanity into more brotherly behaviour than it was the case in the past.

Finally as I have done in my 'Escapism into Landscapism' I feel somehow once more the moral obligation to apologize for a lack of formal education in the field of this engaging knowledge I am writing about. My excuse is coming from the fact that life is too short, and the available time had to be dissipated in other types of preparation, and by the necessity germinated out of unusually gritty vicissitudes. A compassionate excuse is also coming from a rewarding enthusiasm which has been inducive for me to scratch the surface of a garden in making, of past and present landscapes, and now, of different types of gardens. Should I further be permitted the privilege to do so I would certainly and gladly continue the scratching, and you could again be listening to or simply assisting in my writing.

THE END